HUMANISM, WHAT'S THAT?

HUMANISM, WHAT'S THAT?
A Book for Curious Kids

HELEN BENNETT

Prometheus Books

59 John Glenn Drive
Amherst, New York 14228-2197

Published 2005 by Prometheus Books

Inquiries should be addressed to
Prometheus Books
59 John Glenn Drive
Amherst, New York 14228–2197
VOICE: 716–691–0133, ext. 207
FAX: 716–564–2711
WWW.PROMETHEUSBOOKS.COM

09 08 07 06 05   5 4 3 2 1

Library of Congress Cataloging-in-Publication Data

Bennett, Helen, 1937–
    Humanism, what's that? : a book for curious kids / Helen Bennett.
        p. cm.
    Includes bibliographical references.
    ISBN 1–59102–387–4 (pbk.)
    1. Humanism—Juvenile literature. 2. Secular humanism—Juvenile literature. I. Title.

BL2747.6.B46 2005
211'.6—dc22

2004024433

Printed in the United States of America on acid-free paper

For my grandchildren, Aaron, Bryn, and Catie.

In memory of Elaine Rauschal.

CONTENTS

CONTENTS

INTRODUCTION

Not long ago, a teacher named Mrs. Green was teaching a science class of curious kids. These kids loved science, but they were also interested in math, social studies, and just about everything you can think of. They liked to do experiments to find out how things work. A few kids were noisy or unruly, but Mrs. Green didn't mind. She liked to observe their activities and enjoyed their enthusiasm when they learned new things.

One day, the class had terrible news. A popular classmate named Amanda was struck by a car as she was riding her bike to school. Amanda was badly hurt and was taken to the hospital. There she lay in a coma, unable to speak or even see her parents or other visitors. The doctors didn't know if they could save Amanda, as she was so severely injured. The entire school took up a collection to send her flowers, and most of the kids sent cards to her hospital room. A concerned boy named Jesse said to Mrs. Green, "Let's all pray for Amanda. I bet God will make her well if He hears our prayers." Mrs. Green answered, "I'm sorry, Jesse, but we can't do that as a class. If you wish, you may pray on your own, silently, or pray at home or after school."

The students were surprised at Mrs. Green's reply to Jesse's suggestion. Many of the children were sure that they had a right to pray together—then and there—in the classroom. But Mrs. Green explained that it would not be proper for them to pray in class because the United States Constitution assures that there is what some people call a separation of church and state. And so began the conversation that makes up this book.

CHAPTER 1

TO PRAY OR NOT TO PRAY?

Jesse: Why doesn't the government allow us to pray in school? This is not a Communist country! Don't we have freedom here?

Mrs. Green: We certainly do have the freedom to express religious beliefs. Our country has many different groups of people who belong to different religions or they may not hold religious beliefs at all. Some have deep-felt moral beliefs by which they live their lives. Therefore, if even one person doesn't believe in the group's prayer, that student's beliefs must be respected.

Mary: But why can't that person just not pray?

Mrs. Green: Because he or she would feel left out and possibly teased or bullied into going along with the larger group—the majority. Our country was founded on religious freedom—and that includes the right to disagree, or to *hold no religious belief* at all.

Chad: But all good people are religious! They believe in God, and only God can make people well—if we pray hard enough.

Mrs. Green: Sorry, Chad, but not all people agree. Not everyone believes in God, but that doesn't make them bad people.

Jesse: What kind of people do not believe in God? How can they be good if they don't go to church?

Mrs. Green: There are several kinds of nonbelievers. Some are called atheists, while others call themselves agnostics, freethinkers, or humanists. All these people are highly ethical. That means, they believe in doing good because it is the right thing to do, not because they are afraid of God's punishment.

Jesse: Do you believe in God, Mrs. Green?

Mrs. Green: Teachers are not supposed to discuss their beliefs with their students. So what I believe or don't believe is not important here. Teachers must remain "objective" and present all sides of a question so that students can decide for themselves.

Steve: Tell us how people who don't believe in God can be good! I think teachers who don't believe in God should be fired!

Mrs. Green: If you really are curious about a different view, we can meet as a group about it after class if you will get your parent to sign a permission slip. We'll talk about Humanism, an ancient philosophy that many good people follow.

The class took permission slips home and six children (out of thirty-two) were allowed to take Mrs. Green's after-school class on Humanism. When the discussion group met, here is my best recollection of what happened.

Mrs. Green: The people I want to tell you about are called Humanists. I use a capital

"H" when I write about them because they are committed to the Humanist philosophy of life. Other people may be "humanists" with a small "h." They agree with Humanists on many social issues, but may belong to a religion.

Jesse: What do Humanists (with a big "H") believe about God?

Mrs. Green: They believe that God is an idea that people came up with long ago when they were trying to figure out how nature worked and how to get good results when they planted seeds for food. They wanted to avoid acts of nature that could produce disasters.

Jenna: Such as?

Mrs. Green: Such as lightning storms, hurricanes, earthquakes, floods, droughts, famine, sickness—all the bad stuff that can happen that we have no control over. They wanted to have good luck in their hunting, too. They also wanted to win battles with their enemies, just as warring nations do now. People used to believe that all things in nature—such as the wind, the rain, the sun and moon, the animals and plants—had spirits in them that could be controlled through prayer and sacrifice, or giving these spirits what the people thought the spirits wanted. These spirits eventually were named as gods, like the Greek gods of Thunder (Zeus), of Love (Aphrodite), of War (Ares), and of Wisdom (Athena). Each part or activity of human nature was controlled by a god who acted in a very human way. For instance, Zeus was always fighting with his wife, Hera, in much the same way that married couples quarrel. However, some wise men called philosophers did not believe in these gods.

Steve: They were smart! The gods are not like people who fight. There is only *one* God, and you can't see Him. He lives in the sky and sees you all the time.

Mrs. Green: What does he do?

Steve: He writes down in a big book whenever you commit a sin. We all do sins—we were

15

born that way! If you have too many sins, and don't get them forgiven by a priest, you can't get into heaven. You go to hell!

Mary: It doesn't have anything to do with a priest! Some people will go to heaven no matter what they do. They are called the "elected." There's a big election in heaven between God and the angels. Whoever gets the majority vote goes to heaven.

Mrs. Green: When does this happen?

Mary: Before you are born. Before *everyone* is born, the election is held for the whole world.

Joan: That's not what my church says. Our minister told us that Jesus died for our sins. That means *everybody* gets to go to heaven. Even if we sin some more.

Jesse: Don't the Humanists understand Jesus?

Mrs. Green: The Humanists have a different idea here. They do not believe that Jesus was a god, or the son of God. They think he was a great teacher who had many wise things to say, but they don't believe that he was born of a virgin or rose from the dead.

Jesse: Wow! How can you say that? I'll bet all Humanists are Jews!

Mrs. Green: What do you mean, Jesse? Tell us what you know about the Jews.

Jesse: That they are bad people because they killed Jesus. They didn't believe that He was the Messiah!

Mrs. Green: You are right that most Jews didn't believe that Jesus was the Messiah. The Jews thought that an inspired leader, someone they called "the Messiah," would come to rescue them from the Romans, who had taken over their land and were cruel to them. But Jesus didn't fight the Romans, as he spoke of the "Kingdom of God," not the problems here on Earth. The new religion called Christianity believed that Jesus was both the Son of God and God Himself, so that was most important to them.

Jesus himself was a Jew who did not intend to start a new religion. But some Jews felt threatened by Jesus, as he didn't follow all their old rules. The Jewish priests who feared Jesus had him captured and then turned him over to the Roman authorities, who put him to death. Though some thoughtless people accuse all the Jews of killing Jesus, we don't blame people for the sins of their ancestors. Today we try to make amends for a wrong that has been done in the past, such as slavery, but that doesn't mean those living now are actually guilty of the evil. If someone in your family had committed a crime, would you think it fair if you went to jail for it?

Jenna: No! I wouldn't take the rap for something my great-grandma did! She died long before I was born!

Mrs. Green: Exactly! In the Jewish Bible, or the Old Testament as it is called by Christians, God often takes out His anger on people who weren't even there when a crime was committed. He punished the whole human race, except Noah and his family, just because many people—but not all—were, in His view, bad. God had power over everyone and everything, and so, at least according to the Bible, He was often cruel. When someone has unlimited power, it can be misused.

Chad: So you believe that God was wrong? How can that be? He is God after all!

Mrs. Green: If something is good, it is good whether there is a God or not. It does not become good simply because God says so. If we murder someone, isn't that bad? Do we need God to tell us that we would not like to be murdered ourselves? If we are kind to others, and honor our mother and father, is that not good? Doesn't common sense tell us we will be happier if we don't fight and abuse others, but do kind deeds? Should we hurt defenseless animals? We can learn by experience what is the good and right thing to do.

Jenna: But God is always good, isn't that right?

Mrs. Green: The God of the Bible, the one most people in our country believe in, does some things that seem unfair. For example, why would God answer some people's prayers, but not others? Why should God favor one football team over another?

God is seen as a powerful force that is greater than anything we know or could imagine. He is thought to be beyond nature, so He is often described as supernatural. Humanists do not believe in the supernatural. They believe that everything we humans know is a part of nature. It is not God who decides who will live or die, as many people believe. Humanists believe that human beings decide their own futures. We live or die because of our own actions. Some people die because they take chances with their lives—they drive too fast; they smoke too much; they have accidents. Others die of old age or they find out they have a disease.

Joan: But why must everything be a part of nature? Who created nature and the world, if not God?

Mrs. Green: You've heard of the phrase "Mother Nature," haven't you? You know that she is not a real woman. It is a symbol of nature, of our "mother," the Earth. The food, water, and shelter we get from things in nature take care of us, as a mother would care for her children. Just so, God is a symbol of the all-powerful mystery of creation.

Many people believe that our world didn't develop over time but was created by God—you know, the way you create trees and animals and people out of clay during art class. Humanists do not believe that the world was "created" by anyone. The earth and all things on it developed or "evolved" over billions of years.

We humans are all part of the animal kingdom, which grew and developed and changed over the ages, from a single-celled organism—the kind you see under your microscope—to who we are as many-celled human beings. Charles Darwin explained evolution in the nineteenth century, and Humanists and most educated people believe he was right. You will study evolution in your biology class to see how it works.

Chad: But the Bible says that God created man in His own image! And then He created woman out of Adam's rib.

Mrs. Green: Humanists believe just the opposite: that we created God in our image. They believe that the Genesis creation story is a myth, like the Greek myths about gods and goddesses and their efforts to influence how human beings behave. Every culture has its own creation myth. Though there is much wisdom in the Bible, it is a book written by humans, not God, and like other books written by humans it contains mistakes and parts that are confusing. Believers tell us that the Bible is a book that shows us that God loves us, but the Old Testament Book of Proverbs tells parents to beat their children. The New Testament Letter of Paul to the Romans says that those who are "disobedient to parents . . . are worthy of death."

Joan: I can't believe it! My parents would never let me be killed. They would be very sad and cry! They never even spank me. Are they going against God?

Mrs. Green: I don't think so. I just believe they are being humanistic, which is another word for humane.

Chad: You mean, like the Humane Society?

Mrs. Green: Humane means "kind." Humanists believe in kindness toward all people—not just people of one particular group. They believe that human beings must take responsibility for their own actions, and not depend on a God that they don't believe exists.

Mary: If you don't believe in God, you can't get to heaven!

Mrs. Green: Humanists don't believe in heaven either. They believe we should concern ourselves with our life on earth—now! Humanists want to make life better for all people. Since human beings "invented" the gods and the God of the Jews, Christians, and Muslims, their own potential for doing good is unlimited. That means, they can be inventive, brilliant, and solve any problem that life presents, by themselves.

Steve: But why be good if you can't get to heaven?

Mrs. Green: Because Humanists believe that being "good" makes the world better for everyone.

Jenna: What does it mean to be "good"?

Mrs. Green: For a Humanist it means looking at each situation carefully, and considering how your actions will affect not only you, but others. You don't want to harm other people, and you want to help them whenever possible. Therefore, a Humanist would never deliberately bully, tease, or hurt anyone's feelings. If he did that without thinking, he would apologize. Of course, a Humanist would never be violent toward anyone because that would hurt others the most. And a Humanist does not think war is the best way of solving arguments. People must learn to get along by talking and coming to agreements, not by threats or grown-up bullying, which is called war.

Steve: What if other countries want to go to war?

Mrs. Green: If another country begins a war, we must defend ourselves. Everybody has the right to defend themselves if they are threatened. But we must try everything we can to avoid war in the first place. The leaders who declare war do not themselves get killed. It's our young men and women, our hope for the future, who risk their lives and often die in wars. Nothing is worse for a family than to lose a son or daughter.

Joan: If God or the Bible isn't there to show us the way, then how can I know if what I do is right?

Mrs. Green: A Humanist would say that you must consider if your action might hurt someone else. Everyone deserves to be accepted and loved, just as everyone should have enough food, shelter, and clothing. We must all live in a safe world where others care about us and accept us for who we are.

Mary: But killing is wrong, isn't it? So abortion must be wrong, too.

Mrs. Green: All of you know how babies come into the world, right? I don't need to explain before answering Mary's question, do I?

The Group: We know!

Mrs. Green: Good. Well, Humanists usually support a woman's right to choose what to do with her own body, especially in the first three months of her pregnancy. They believe that the fetus only becomes a person after it is born. If someone kills a baby after it is born, that would be murder. But when the fetus is still an embryo—you know what that is—in the very early stages of development, it is up to the woman to follow her conscience. If she chooses to give birth to the baby, she can decide to keep the child herself or she could ask that it be adopted by adults who will love it. Or, she could decide to stop the pregnancy from progressing to birth. If abortion is made illegal, many women will die as unqualified people perform abortions on them.

Jenna: But why is that not murder, if you kill an unborn baby? It is a human, isn't it?

Mrs. Green: Many Humanists believe that a fetus, although human, is not yet a person. Many agree with Andrew Johnson, who wrote in the magazine *Free Inquiry*, ". . . an embryo, or a fetus is not a person. It is for this reason that the rights of a pregnant woman—who is a person—to privacy, to equality, and to control of her body prevail by right and must continue to prevail by law." A woman is considered a person, not just a "human," because she has moral responsibilities as well as rights. She can judge the difference between right and wrong, but a fetus is not aware of such things. That means that a woman's right to control her own body is most important here.

Chad: So Humanists believe in women's rights?

Mrs. Green: Of course! Women must be treated equally and given the same opportunities as men.

Steve: Don't you think that boys are stronger than girls? That boys shouldn't cry? That's what my dad says.

Mrs. Green: Many people would disagree with your dad. Boys usually have more physical strength, but girls are more aware of their emotions. Both boys and girls must be able to express their emotions freely. If they hold their feelings in, they may get more and more anger inside which may later make them feel confused, or it could make them want to lash out and hit someone. We need to rely on both reason and emotion to live a balanced life. Reason means thinking things out clearly. Emotion concerns our feelings.

CHAPTER 2

WHAT ABOUT AMANDA?

Joan: We're forgetting about Amanda. She is still in the hospital and can't talk. How will she get better without prayer?

Mrs. Green: The doctors will do all they can for her. Nurses will take care of her night and day, and the love of her parents, relatives, and friends will be there to help her. She will *feel* their love as they sit beside her, hold her hand, and talk to her.

Jesse: But what if she dies anyway? Shouldn't we ask God to save her?

Mrs. Green: If it makes you feel better, pray by yourself or with your friends. Humanists believe that if she gets better, we should thank Amanda's doctors, nurses, and parents. They are the ones taking care of her. Science has discovered many new medicines and ways to help make people better. To some these treatments are like "miracles." But still, even with all the medicines and such, Amanda might die.

Joan: Why would God do that to her? She's just a little kid, like us.

Mrs. Green: Perhaps the Humanists are right here and God is not responsible. After the medicine and other treatments are tried we sometimes have to wait for our bodies to start healing on their own—you know, like when you cut your knee and it heals after a while. No one is punishing Amanda or her parents.

Jenna: What will happen to Amanda if she dies? Will she go to heaven?

Mrs. Green: Humanists don't think so. Since they don't believe that God exists, there isn't any heaven or hell, except the ideas we have of these places in our heads. Amanda's heaven—the place she will live forever—will be in your memory. The love her friends have for her will last long after she is no longer here to talk and play with us. Of course, you can put together a book of memories to record her ideas and all the kind things she did. You can have a memorial service to remember her with love. Amanda will never be forgotten because her thoughts and actions have changed the way other people think and act. We are all connected, and we all affect one another.

Joan: She helped me with my homework.

Steve: She was a good sport!

Jenna: Amanda had a beautiful smile and was always kind.

Mary: Do Humanists believe we will live forever?

Mrs. Green: Just as I said, we will live in the memories of those who knew us. The things we did will live on after our death. Even people born in the future, who didn't personally know her, will be affected by

Amanda through the friends she left behind whose lives were changed by her.

Steve: So what can we do to help her?

Mrs. Green: You can hope she recovers. You can send notes to her parents to show how much you care. You can pray or meditate, if you wish. To meditate is to think good thoughts about her. But the best thing you can do is to become a more caring person. Do this for Amanda and yourself. Then you will live on forever, too.

Joan: Do Humanists go to church?

Mrs. Green: Not the usual churches. Humanists, like everyone else, often get together to discuss their ideas and interact with one another. So they form organizations and associations, like the American Humanist Association, which has branches almost everywhere. Humanists may have regular meetings and annual gatherings, or some may not belong to any organization at all. Some belong to the Ethical Culture Society, which is like a religion, but without a god. It supports good works that make people's lives better: for example, helping the homeless or trying to free someone from prison who was falsely accused of a crime. An established religion that practices humanist principles and has many Humanists among its members is Unitarian Universalism. Unitarian Universalists believe, as do Humanists, in the "inherent worth and dignity of every person." That means that everyone is born good and has equal value as a human being. They also believe in science, democracy, reason, and the "interdependent web" of which we are all a part.

Mary: "Inter-deepended" what?

Mrs. Green: Many Humanists believe that all things in the world—all people, animals, plants, rocks and stones, and everything else—are connected to one another. If an endangered species of animal dies out, we are all affected. If people are sick and starving in any part of the world, we must help them because we are all brother and sister human beings. If we ignore those in need, the world will become a very dangerous place where people desperate for food, water, and a place to live will risk harming others to stay alive.

Chad: Is that what happened in the September 11 attack on America?

Mrs. Green: Perhaps that is partly the cause. Some people believe we should be at war if we do not share the same beliefs and political systems. Many people do not have a good education, a good job, or hope for the future, and so they think it is better to kill themselves and go to what they believe to be heaven rather than to work out our differences and live in brotherhood and tolerance. Suicide bombers are people who have little to believe in except their "cause," which is to have their own religion and way of life prevail. They may be unaware of the concept of individual freedom, that is, freedom to worship and live one's own life in the way one chooses. They care nothing about democracy, which helps people choose their own leaders and come together to create their own laws.

Jenna: What can we do?

Mrs. Green: We can refuse to hate our enemies. We must try to help them resolve their problems, but at the same time not let them destroy our freedom of thought and our belief in equality of opportunity for all.

Mary: It sounds hard to do all that.

Mrs. Green: That's why it is so important to learn as much as possible about our world—its languages, its people, and its science, religion, and art. The more informed we are, the more we know about the world, the better we will be able to solve our problems. Humanists believe that no supernatural God will solve them for us. We must do all we can to find solutions ourselves by using all our abilities and special skills. Each of us has something to contribute to this great task.

Steve: How can we be sure we will live on after we die?

Mrs. Green: We are all connected. Each of us is like a cell in a very huge body that makes up the world. So when we die, the rest of that body lives on. Each of us should want to live our lives in such a way that when we die those who remain will be happier and the earth will be better because we were in the world. We would never want to hurt our own body, so we must never hurt any part of the world. We must cherish the earth and keep it clean and beautiful, just as we must care for all human beings and animals.

Mary: My minister says that my church knows the truth, and all the other churches are wrong. Is he right?

Mrs. Green: All of us want to believe that the ideas we have about the world and the way we should live are the correct ones. No one wants to believe that they could be wrong in their beliefs. Religious groups are no different. Many of them have the view that there is *only one* possible way to view the world and that is God's way. And since each of these religions believes that its is the correct view of God's way, then of course all the others will be viewed as wrong. It is this kind of thinking that caused many religions and countries to go to war over who was really right. Many, many people throughout history suffered and died because the various religions couldn't admit that they might be wrong.

The fact is, *no one person or religion* really knows the whole truth—and that includes Humanists! It is impossible to know the whole and complete truth, as our senses are limited, and everyone's personal experience is also limited to himself or herself.

Jesse: I know what I see! I hear what I hear! What do you mean, "limited"?

Mrs. Green: Suppose you have an eye infection or weak ears. You have seen people wearing hearing aids and glasses, haven't you? People who have faulty senses may not observe the world the way the rest of us do. In fact, everyone sees, hears, smells, tastes, and touches things differently. You may like one food, and I may prefer another. How can we all agree?

Mary: What if someone goes blind?

Mrs. Green: Helen Keller was both blind and deaf from an early age. She perceived the world differently from the way we do, but she was still able to learn.

The best hope for an agreement on "truth" is science.

Mary: Do scientists believe in God?

Mrs. Green: Some do and some do not. It depends on how one defines "God."

Jesse: What do you mean, "defines God"? I thought everyone knows who God is.

Mrs. Green: No, it's not that easy. Many different views of God exist—as many as there are people on this planet, I suppose. We must first define what we mean before we say if we believe it. God can be "love" for some, a "divine" spark inside us for others, or something/someone out there dominating the universe, for those who read the Bible literally.

Jenna: What do you mean by reading the Bible literally?

Mrs. Green: For some people the Bible means exactly what it says! There really was an Eden and an Adam and Eve created by God, who were parents to us all. Or that God spoke to Moses through a burning bush. If we read the Bible "figuratively," it means that parts of it are myths having meaning for us based on our interpretations. The Bible should be admired for the lessons it teaches rather than being the written word of God.

Steve: Mrs. Green, do you read the Bible literally?

Mrs. Green: I will tell you how Humanists interpret the Bible. They think that most of it is myth, mixed in with some history.

But there is also truth in mythology, just as there are truths to be found in fairy tales and fables.

Steve: What???

Mrs. Green: Cinderella may never have really existed, but she stands for all girls who dream of being rescued by a handsome "prince." She is a symbol. Aesop told tales about animals, such as the hare and the tortoise, which had symbolic meaning. Being slow is not bad as long as you get the job done! Just so, Adam and Eve are symbols of early humans trying to figure out their place in the world. And Santa Claus is a symbol of human kindness. Ooops! I didn't mean to spill the beans on Santa!

Kids: We knew that already! Do you think we're dummies? We're not babies!

Mrs. Green: Then you may be ready to hear that some people believe that God is like Santa Claus! God is a symbol of everything humans wish for and would like to be: eternal, loving, good, giving, spiritual, free, all-powerful, immortal, and all the other things we yearn for.

Some people call themselves atheists because they believe that no good evidence for the existence of God has been offered by those who claim God does exist. Agnostics don't know if there is a god or not. They are still unsure and so they keep looking for evidence one way or the other. Humanists, who may be atheists or agnostics, feel sure that human beings can make the world better.

Jenna: So I'll bet you believe in God as a symbol, Mrs. Green.

Mrs. Green: Well, if I were a Humanist I would perhaps believe that God is a symbol of our highest ideals. I would also believe that God is a metaphor for the mystery of the unknowable. A metaphor is something that stands for an idea. But since it is hard to pray to a symbol or a metaphor, Humanists just meditate and try to do good.

Mary: Are Humanists religious?

Mrs. Green: I prefer to think of some of them as spiritual. "Spiritual" refers to those things we enjoy at the highest level. For the religious, this usually means the worship of God. Many Humanists are satisfied to live their beliefs by supporting causes that have good consequences for society. Others need spirituality in their lives, which they define for themselves. Since most Humanists do not believe in a separable soul, or spirit, that leaves the body after death, their spirituality may be confined to experiences of connection with the universe, or the love of nature, art, music, literature, or humanity. Many humanists are called religious humanists because they are part of some group, such as *Unitarian Universalism* or *Humanistic Judaism*, which consists of people who wish to preserve their Jewish heritage, but without belief in the supernatural, or the God of their Bible. Most are *secular* humanists, meaning that they are not part of any church or religion.

Jenna: Where did Humanism come from? Weren't Humanists afraid of the gods, like other people?

Mrs. Green: Humanism started long ago, possibly in ancient Greece. Some scientists and thinkers doubted the existence of the gods. They looked to nature and their five senses to help explain how the world works. They tested their ideas with experiments—the beginnings of modern science. We know that the ancient Greek Protagoras was one of the first Humanists. He said, "Man is the measure of all things." This means we perceive the world through our own eyes, so we are most important. We created the gods ourselves. Other Greek Humanists were important thinkers like the Sophists, Socrates, Plato, and Aristotle.

Jenna: What happened to Humanism then?

Mrs. Green: During the Dark Ages—remember this period of time from your history books—Humanism was largely forgotten, as the Catholic Church took control of daily life. Humanism returned during the Renaissance, when Church doctrine began to be questioned, and the earlier ideas of ancient Greece and Rome in art, science, and philosophy were rediscovered. Some great Humanists (sometimes called "freethinkers") since the Renaissance include Erasmus, Benedict Spinoza, Giordano Bruno, René Descartes, Sir Francis Bacon, John Locke, David Hume, Jeremy Bentham, Voltaire, James Mill, and John Stuart Mill. In America, we had Thomas Paine, Thomas Jefferson, and Robert Ingersoll. Many twentieth-century philosophers, scientists, and writers have been Humanists, including Bertrand Russell, Corliss Lamont, Gerald Larue, Carl Sagan, Kurt Vonnegut, and Isaac Asimov.

Jesse: So it's not just a few kooks?

Mrs. Green: I don't think I'd call them kooks, Jesse. More than a few brave people were burned at the stake or otherwise condemned by society for having the courage to think for themselves and voice their views openly.

Spinoza was a learned Jewish man who was banned from his religion for his belief, called pantheism, that God was in everything. Religious people believed that God created nature, and was not part of it. Giordano Bruno was burned at the stake for challenging the authority of the Catholic Church because he thought that each person's truth may be different. Michael Servetus was also burned because he didn't accept the Trinity, the belief that God has three parts: the Father, the Son, and the Holy Spirit. This happened at a time known as the Inquisition, when the Catholic Church often punished those who disagreed with its teachings.

Of course, most everyone has heard of Joan of Arc. Though she was not a Humanist, she was burned for daring to think for herself. Five hundred years later, the Church admitted it had made a mistake and declared her a saint. The great astronomer Galileo was persecuted by the Church for his accurate beliefs about the stars and the position of the planets. That the Earth was not the center of the universe was hard for religion to swallow. Eventually, most religions accepted the proofs of science. However, there is still some controversy over Darwin's "Theory of Evolution."

Jenna: Is it true? Did we come from monkeys?

Mrs. Green: There is plenty of evidence to support the fact that humans evolved from some lower form of primate. When scientists find fossils in rocks and then study the ages of those rocks, it is apparent that the earth is billions—not thousands—of years old. Just as the sun is at the center of the solar system, and the earth is round, not flat, someday (we hope) all religions will agree with Darwin on evolution.

Jesse: The Bible says Eve is responsible for all human suffering and sin. Is this true?

Mrs. Green: That does women a great injustice. If Eve symbolically ate the fruit of the Tree of the Knowledge of Good and Evil, she was trying to satisfy her hunger for knowledge and to share this benefit with her husband, Adam. Knowledge is never bad; that's why you are in school. Only by knowing the difference between good and evil can we make intelligent choices.

CHAPTER 3

CAN I BE A HUMANIST?

Jesse: Can I be a Humanist?

Mrs. Green: You should know about all your choices and then choose your beliefs wisely, when you are grown up. But anyone of any religion can live by humanistic values.

Jesse: What is the difference between humanistic values and religious values?

Mrs. Green: Humanistic values and religious values have a lot in common. Humanists believe in doing good and helping others, and they respect all living things. But they differ in that Humanists are more tolerant of views not their own. They would never go to war over which view about a god was the "right" one. They also are more accepting of diverse lifestyles than are orthodox religions. That means that they believe that all human beings have value and the right to live as they choose, as long as they do no harm to others. Humanists do not believe in a personal God or "savior." They take responsibility for their own actions and their own lives here on earth.

Steve: But don't they have special rules or laws or religious rituals?

Mrs. Green: Only those they decide for themselves, to make a better world. They try to save the earth as well as all its people, and they are tolerant of others' beliefs. To be a humane and loving person is to have humanistic values.

Jenna: Do Humanists have priests, ministers, or rabbis?

Mrs. Green: Only if they belong to a church or synagogue. Otherwise, they rely on electing officers of their own organizations.

Some humanists don't even know that they are humanists. They simply stand up for justice and work to make society better.

Joan: Will I meet my grandma in heaven after I die?

Mrs. Green: That depends on where you think heaven is. Humanists do not believe that heaven is a place where we go after we die. If you have your grandma in your heart, always, she is there with you already.

Mary: Do Humanists celebrate holidays? What about Christmas and Easter?

Mrs. Green: Of course, Humanists may celebrate holidays. They may think of Christmas as a season of peace and goodwill, and Easter as a season of rebirth, when both the earth and hope are reborn with the spring. Is there anything more beautiful than seeing new leaves on the trees, and blossoms and flowers everywhere after a long, cold winter? Humanists may remember Jesus during these holidays, as his wisdom and kindness will never die. Humanistic Jews would celebrate Passover as a festival of freedom, a time of hope that all humankind will someday be free. Many Humanists and others celebrate the winter solstice, just before Christmas. That's when the days will get longer and spring is on the way. Be the best human being you can be; then you will be a humanist.

Joan: You said we should be the best we can be. But what should I be when I grow up?

Mrs. Green: You should try out many different activities while you are young. It doesn't matter if you're not "the best" at them—as long as you try. Because we are human we make mistakes but we also learn from them. When you find out what you really love to do—do that! You should make a career out of following your heart's desire, and you will love your life.

Jesse: Why did you become a teacher?

Mrs. Green: Because I love to learn. When I grew up, I found out that I learn more by teaching than any other way. I learn from all of you, all the time. But sometimes I think that I'm not that good at it. I lack patience.

Jesse: Don't doctors need patients, too?

Mrs. Green: Yes, but it's spelled differently. Doctors need both kinds, patience to answer people's questions and to reassure them, and patients whom they help get better.

Steve: My dad wants me to be a doctor because there's a lot of money in it.

Mary: Would a Humanist be a doctor?

Mrs. Green: It's possible. But she (or he) wouldn't be in that profession just for the money. She would want to help people first. The money would follow—but then, she might open a clinic in a poor neighborhood to treat those who can't afford to pay for care.

Mary: Can I be a nurse?

Mrs. Green: You can be anything you would like. A woman can be anything a man can be—except a father. You might want to be a doctor or a medical researcher instead of a nurse, or an emergency rescue person. But if you really want to be a nurse, sure, go ahead. Boys can be nurses, too.

Jesse: My dad says I should take over the family's pet food business when I grow up. What do you think?

Mrs. Green: I think you should follow your heart—and your talent. Everyone has a special talent. When you grow up, you should use that talent to become a better and happier person. Then you can make the world better, because you will have more self-respect and pride in your achievements.

Joan: But if we buy lots of nice things, and live in the best houses, won't that make us feel better about ourselves?

Mrs. Green: Perhaps temporarily. But in the long run, what makes people truly happy is the good they can do for others, not how many possessions they have.

Jenna: Do Humanists have their own Bible?

Mrs. Green: Not exactly. But there are three Humanist Manifestos that explain the Humanist vision for the world. I have written a "Humanist Creed" that I'd like to share with you. Here is a copy to take home and study. Let's go over it first.

Humanist Creed

I am the center of my universe;
There is no one else quite like me.
I am part of the human species,
All who came before me and all who will come
    after.
I have things in common with all humankind:
Needs, drives, emotions, intelligence, and a thirst
    for knowledge.
As long as my species survives, I shall never die.
I have no need for a Greater Being to take care of
    me. While that would be nice, it is my respon-
    sibility to take care of myself.
Human beings strive to be good because we need
    to live in peace and harmony, not because we
    fear God.

We create meaning and a plan for our own lives.
It is up to us to follow our plan, or change it
when necessary. We are not godlike, but we
can imagine God. By imagining this perfect
ideal, we can strive to live up to it.

All we need do is to use our intelligence, exercise
our goodwill, and have the courage to continu-
ally strive for our goals.

*After discussing this "Creed," the children were a bit
puzzled.*

Jesse: Do Humanists think we are better
than animals? I would trust my dog more
than many humans I know! My mom says
that animals have rights, too.

Mrs. Green: You are right! We are not the
best species on earth in every way! But we
are the only ones—as far as we know—
who can think, plan, and create a better
world. We can imagine the future and plan
for it. We can even imagine our own deaths
and try to live better lives so that we will
be remembered kindly.

Mary: Mrs. Green, do you really think all people are equal?

Mrs. Green: They are equal in dignity and rights. However, they are far from equal in abilities, intelligence, and understanding. You know that some of you are better at sports, math, or language arts than others. We all have our special talents. Someday, you should read a story called "Harrison Bergeron," which makes fun of the idea of human equality. It was written by a Humanist satirist, Kurt Vonnegut.

Mary: What happens in the story?

Mrs. Green: The story is set a hundred years in the future. The government tries to make all people equal by giving ridiculous "handicaps" to anyone who is smarter, stronger, or more beautiful than anyone else. Everyone is made dumber instead of smarter. We must try to avoid letting this ever happen by recognizing and rewarding excellence. Everyone has different talents and should be encouraged to develop them, as I said before.

Chad: Do you think that criminals have the same rights as everyone else?

Mrs. Green: They have a right to a fair trial and to be treated with dignity. No one should ever be tortured, under any circumstances. The right thing to do would be to try to rehabilitate rather than punish criminals, that is, to teach them how to respect themselves and society. Teach them a trade or vocation so that they have a chance to succeed honestly when they get out of prison.

Jesse: Should murderers get the death penalty?

Mrs. Green: Most Humanists would say no. Sometimes the wrong person is found guilty. Witnesses can be mistaken, or sometimes the law is blinded by prejudice. Prejudice means that we form a bad opinion of someone without actually knowing him or her. But even if the right person is convicted, to kill him or her is to commit the same crime as the murderer. "Two wrongs don't make a right."

Chad: What is the worst crime?

Mrs. Green: I believe the worst crime is bigotry—hating someone just because he or she belongs to another group, race, religion, nationality, or the like, without knowing that person at all. If we can eliminate bigotry and prejudice—and that's a big "if"—we would wipe out the major flaw that keeps our world from becoming a truly happy place.

Joan: And what's the second-worst crime?

Mrs. Green: Perhaps *ignorance*, or not knowing due to lack of education. *Ignorance* may lead to overpopulation, which can lead to war, famine, and poverty, and every other problem humanity faces. To avoid ignorance, go to school, *and keep an open mind!* A closed mind is a wasted mind, and as the saying goes, "A mind is a terrible thing to waste."

Jesse: How should we act? What should we do to make the world better?

Mrs. Green: Be kind. Be compassionate. Put yourself in the other person's shoes and imagine how he or she feels. Then treat him or her as you would wish to be treated. It's just the good old "Golden Rule" that most religions teach.

Joan: It's good to be kind. But can a person be a Humanist and believe in God?

Mrs. Green: Yes. Some Humanists do believe in God. The late actor and comedian Steve Allen did, and he was a wonderful Humanist. In addition to being one of the funniest comics ever, he wrote many brilliant books. He taught that one must question all things and then come to a conclusion based on evidence and reason. His reason led him to a belief in God. Allen said that he was among the majority of people who assume that a god does exist, but he insisted that we apply critical thinking to our beliefs. In other words, we should always test and check our beliefs to make sure we have good reasons for believing as we do. Other Humanists do not accept this idea of God, but they do agree to be tolerant of other people's beliefs.

I have an assignment for you: write a one-line epitaph for different kinds of humanists. An epitaph is a line that we would like to be remembered by, often written on a gravestone. Here is a sample epitaph: "She was a teacher. She was a humanist."

The following are some of the epitaphs the students submitted. See if you can write some more yourself.

"He helped the poor. He was a humanist."

"She was a nurse. She was a humanist."

"She went to Congress. She was a humanist."

"She wrote a new symphony. She was a humanist."

"He was a lawyer who helped the disadvantaged. He was a humanist."

"She was a good wife and mother. She was a humanist."

"He told me he was proud of me. He was a good father. He was a humanist."

To develop your creativity; to express yourself in writing, music, art, sports, science, or any other field; and do good deeds for yourself and society, is to be a humanist. To avoid bigotry, hatred, and bullying is to be a humanist. To tolerate all religious beliefs and people of all "races" is to be a humanist. To live to your full potential and to do good in the world is to be a humanist. You can be a humanist whether you belong to any of the world's religions, or to no religion at all.

Are you a humanist?

POETRY

I Believe

I believe
That we are here to make this world
A better place.
That in order to do so
We must erase
Every trace
Of bigotry and greed.
We must help to meet
Every need
Of those around us.
Our blessings come
From knowing that this earth
That is our home
Is home to all the other parts
That comprise our body.
For we are but a cell

HUMANISM, WHAT'S THAT?

In the vast universe in which we dwell
A little while. But other cells
Regenerate and grow
And all are part
Of that great organism.
The heart
Supplies the central love that keeps
It going,
And the brain supplies the compass
And the map,
Bestowing
On all the world
Unending joy and bliss,
When we perceive our transient lives
Like this.

Kindness

With all of the natural causes of grief:
Disease and death, famine and war,
Accidents that destroy a life
That was filled with vigor and joy before;
With all of the cruel tricks of fate,
Whose whim we are all at the mercy of,
Why do we add to that pitiless sum
When we could bind up our wounds with love?
Why is unkindness so prevalent?
Why is compassion so weak and rare?
Why do we spout insincere clichés,
Pretending we're people who really care?
The kindness we fail to extend each day
To everybody who crosses our path
Is a frown we carry inside our hearts,
Filling our souls with remorse and wrath.
But a deed of compassion and empathy,
A kindness spoken and acted on,
Will engage us with immortality,
And reverberate when we are gone.

I'm Glad I'm Not a Bigot

I'm glad I'm not a bigot,
My heart's a hate-free zone,
But if I were a bigot I wouldn't be alone.
I'd have disgraceful company
Like the KKK,
I'm glad I'm not a bigot,
I wasn't born that way.

If I were a bigot
I wouldn't try to stem
My tendency to see the world
As simply "us" and "them."
Those folks who seem subhuman
For vengeful deeds are ripe,
And every ethnic group would be
Reduced to stereotype.

A bully is a bigot
Who picks on girls and boys,
He always fights with smaller kids;
A bully just destroys
His chances to be popular,
For, tough as he may seem,
A bully's just a coward
Who's lacking self-esteem.

I'm glad I'm not a bigot
For here is what I'd miss:
The chance to love and laugh and know
The broadest kind of bliss.
For we are likelier to find
A joy that never ends,
The broader our acquaintance,
The more diverse our friends.

Humanist Hymn

We believe the Master Plan
For the betterment of man
Is designed by us alone,
For we reap what we have sown.

We don't need a deity
To grant us immortality;
By our actions, we alone
Make our names forever known.

We are not here to rehearse
Our place in the universe;
From the moment of our birth
We belong to Planet Earth.

All the trees and mountains tall,
All the creatures great and small
Of this ever-twirling ball
Heeded evolution's call.

All the wonders of our world
Into human hands are hurled;
Science is our tool to know
How to heal and how to grow.

Let's design a better land
All together, and demand
Freedom and equality,
Inborn worth and dignity.

Every woman, every man
Has the power, and we can
Make a tattered world like this
Ring with rapture, sing with bliss.

Let us all join hands and stand
In a circle large and grand,
As together we devise
Our own earthly paradise.

Thank You, Life

Thank you, Life
For each good thing,
For air to breathe,
For songs to sing.
For kites to fly,
For food to eat,
For friends to love,
For running feet.

Thank you, Life
For swings to swing,
For games to play,
For everything.
And when I'm grown
I know I'll be
Thankful still
That I am me.

What Humanism Means to Me

Humanism means to me
I've got the opportunity
To realize that I am free
To take responsibility.

To me, it doesn't seem so odd
That many people pray to God
Whenever they are feeling low—
It's just the way they have to go.

But when I do not know the way
I do not feel the need to pray.
I use my brain to figure out
What the problem's all about.

I'm grateful that I have my eyes
To see the beauty of the skies,
I'm glad I have my ears to hear
The voices of my friends so dear.

But best of all, my brain's the one
That figures out what must be done
To help me run a better race,
To make the world a better place.

ACTIVITIES AND DISCUSSION QUESTIONS

Activities

1. Draw a picture of a "Happy Humanist." (A "Happy Humanist" is the emblem of the American Humanist Association.) Under the picture, explain why he or she is happy.

2. Write a story with a humanist hero or heroine.

3. Write a poem, a song, or an essay about humanism.

4. Write a letter to your local paper about an issue that concerns you. Send it in for publication.

5. Write a letter to your state or federal representative or senator about a law he or she is considering. Explain why you want this law passed or

defeated. Be sure to include your name, address, and age.

6. Try to find a pen pal in another country and establish a friendship through the mail or by e-mail.

7. Consider having your group or family sponsor an underprivileged child in a foreign country through an agency such as Children International. You would pay a small monthly fee to help this child get the necessities of life.

8. Form a humanist group with your peers. Consider joining a Humanist association.

9. Read books by humanist authors and study humanistic philosophers as you continue to grow. (See Bibliography)

Discussion Questions

1. Humanism is a *positive* philosophy that asserts the potential for goodness in every human being. How does this contrast with the

religious doctrine of "original sin"? ("Original sin" means we were all born bad.)

2. Humanism affirms the equality of man and woman. How would you raise your sons and daughters to ensure that they grow up as equals?

3. Why are good manners important to humanists? Why should you obey school rules?

4. What would you do if you saw someone bullying another student?

5. If someone brought a gun to school, or boasted that he was going to do so, would you tell someone? Who? Why?

6. Compare Humanism with Christianity, Judaism, Buddhism, Islam, or any other world religion that you have studied. How do they differ? How are they similar?

7. How would you behave if your team won a championship? Would you thank God? Why or why not?

8. How would you react if you lost a game or failed a test? Whose fault would it be?

9. A fanatic is someone who goes to extremes, even when he may be wrong about something. For example, a suicide bomber is considered a fanatic by most people. How can we oppose fanaticism, while still valuing the inborn worth and dignity of the fanatic?

10. If your country drafted you to fight in a war (and you were old enough), what would you do?

11. Since you are tolerant of all beliefs, what would you do if people were treated unjustly in the name of their religion? Can you think of examples of unfair treatment of women and children in other cultures? Do we have the right to interfere with such treatment?

12. How can we in America come to cherish diversity (differences among people) and overcome prejudice, hatred, and violence?

13. Which TV programs should we boycott—not watch—because they promote poor values?

(Poor values are those that are unethical, that hurt people or fail to respect them.) What are these poor values? What can be done about such programs?

14. Humanism is opposed to violence. Which video games promote violence? Do you think you should play such games? Why or why not?

15. We should be the best we can be and not bow to peer pressure. That happens when friends try to convince us to do something we know is bad for us. What would you do if someone offered you cigarettes, drugs, or alcohol at a party?

16. We should respect all human beings, as we are all alike in dignity and worth. If you are a humanist, how would you behave responsibly on a date?

17. Which will make a better world, competition or cooperation? How much of each of these things is good? Should we be more concerned with our individuality or belonging to a group?

18. What do you think of school uniforms? Should you have the freedom to express your individuality, or do uniforms promote better behavior and equality of opportunity among students? Why do some grown-ups think that students should wear uniforms?

19. Why do young people follow fashion? Should you always try to keep up with the "in crowd," or find your own style?

20. Many organizations work to eliminate bad conditions in the world. Some examples are Amnesty International, which opposes torture; the Southern Poverty Law Center, which opposes bigotry with its *Teaching Tolerance* magazine; Habitat for Humanity, which builds houses for poor people; Planned Parenthood, which promotes responsible parenthood; and such groups as the World Wildlife Fund, Greenpeace, and the Sierra Club, which safeguard the environment. UNICEF helps the world's children, and the Humane Society protects pets. What can you personally do to help people, animals, and the environment?

SELECTED BIBLIOGRAPHY
FOR OLDER TEENS AND ADULTS

Allen, Steve. *"Dumbth": The Lost Art of Thinking.* Amherst, NY: Prometheus Books, 1989.

————. *Steve Allen on the Bible, Religion, and Morality.* Amherst, NY: Prometheus Books, 1990.

Ingersoll, Robert. *The Best of Robert Ingersoll: Immortal Infidel: Selections from His Writings and Speeches.* Edited by Roger E. Greeley. Amherst, NY: Prometheus Books, 1983.

Lamont, Corliss. *The Philosophy of Humanism.* New York: Continuum, 1993.

Russell, Bertrand. *The Basic Writings of Bertrand Russell.* Edited by Robert E. Egner and Lester E. Denonn. New York: Simon and Schuster, 1961.

Sagan, Carl, and Ann Druyan. *Shadows of Forgotten Ancestors: A Search for Who We Are.* New York: Ballantine Books, 1992.